Chinese through Tone & Color

Nathan Dummitt

Hippocrene Books
New York

Book design and illustrations by Dan Acton

For information, address:
Hippocrene Books, Inc.
171 Madison Avenue
New York, NY 10016
www.hippocrenebooks.com

Library of Congress Cataloging-in-Publication Data

Dummitt, Nathan.
    Chinese through tone & color / Nathan Dummitt
        p.cm.
    Chinese and English. Includes index.
    ISBN-13: 978-0-7818-1204-7 (alk. paper)
    ISBN-10: 0-7818-1204-6 (alk. paper)
        1. Chinese language--Textbooks for foreign speakers--English.
    I.Title. II. Title: Chinese through tone and color.

    PL1129.E5D862007
    495--dc22

                                            2007061360

Printed and bound in China.

CONTENTS

I would like to thank Dan Acton for his assistance with the book, and Yong Ho for his extremely helpful comments and corrections. Any mistakes that remain are my own.

I would also like to acknowledge three wonderful teachers and colleagues of mine for their support and inspiration: Issei Ogawa, Marvin Terban and Joanie Dean.

Mandarin Chinese is a tonal language. This means that a single spoken syllable, such as "ti," can have at least four different meanings depending on the tone in which it is spoken.

踢	*to kick*	FIRST TONE ► tī
提	*to lift*	SECOND TONE ► tí
体	*body*	THIRD TONE ► tǐ
替	*to replace*	FOURTH TONE ► tì

Many speakers of non-tonal languages find this to be the most difficult aspect of mastering Chinese. In fact, it is possible to write an entire poem in Chinese using just one syllable. Zhao Yuanren, an extremely influential Chinese linguist in the 20th century, composed a 10-line classical Chinese poem using only the sound *shi* repeated 92 times in all four tones. While the poem is somewhat nonsensical when read, and completely incomprehensible when only heard, it illustrates the large and confusing potential afforded by a tonal language.

<施氏食狮史>

石室诗士施氏，嗜狮，誓食十狮。
施氏时时适市视狮。
十时，适十狮适市。
是时，适施氏适市。
氏视是十狮，恃矢势，使是十狮逝世。
氏拾是十狮尸，适石室。
石室湿，氏使侍拭石室。
石室拭，氏始试食是十狮。
食时，始识是十狮，实十石狮尸。
试释是事。

2

The Lion-Eating Poet in the Stone Den

Shi, the poet who loved to eat lions, lived in a stone den.
He swore to eat ten lions, and went to the market every day to look for them.
One day at 10 o'clock, ten lions happened to come to the market.
Shi arrived at the market too just at that time,
Seeing the ten lions, he killed them with arrows.
He brought the corpses of the ten lions to the stone den.
The den was damp, so he had his servant wipe it.
When the den was wiped, he tried to eat the lions.
When he ate, he realized that the ten lions were actually ten corpses.
Try to explain this!

Curious readers can find a reading of this poem at the end of disc 2.

In Pinyin romanization (the official phonetic translation of Chinese into the Roman alphabet), these four tones are distinguished by the following respective marks:

—　　　　　　ˊ　　　　　　ˇ　　　　　　ˋ

However, this tone indication is placed only above the romanization of the words, not above the characters themselves. This book was written to expose the learner to the written Chinese language while simultaneously providing an intuitive method to learn and pronounce the words in the correct tone quickly and easily.

Numerous books have been written on the origin, stroke order, and proper writing of Chinese characters, or hanzi. The main focus of this book is on tone and character recognition. Characters have been selected primarily on the basis of their usage frequency in written and spoken Chinese. Common but more complicated grammatical constructions have been omitted in favor of words that will be more useful to the beginning student.

The characters are presented in a clean and simple manner, starting with the basic words (I, you, speak, Chinese) that the beginning learner is likely to encounter. Since there is no grammatical inflection in Chinese, it is possible to construct hundreds of well-formed sentences with the first 15 or so characters.

While this book introduces a little over one hundred hanzi, it does not in fact deal with only one hundred words. Mandarin Chinese has developed into a primarily disyllabic language, in which most words are composed of two characters. Though most of the entries in this book exist as individual nouns and verbs, some of the most common characters have slightly different meanings when combined with other characters or when used in different contexts. For this reason, the translations given for individual characters are meant to be an introduction to the character's most general meaning, rather than an exhaustive catalog of all possible uses. As your study of the language progresses, you will discover new meanings and uses for even the most basic characters.

When used in conjunction with a good dictionary, this book will speed your acquisition of both written and spoken Mandarin. While you do not need to read the entire book from cover to cover, it is best to familiarize yourself with the color-assignment system before studying specific characters. When the book is read in order, color Romanized pronunciation is included for characters that have not been introduced yet, and words that are not covered in the book are left as colored Romanization throughout.

In addition to the English Word Index at the back of the book, there is also an index organized by color, should you encounter a character you do not know.

Each of the four tones in Mandarin Chinese has been assigned a color:

1ST TONE RED: HIGH AND LEVEL
2ND TONE ORANGE: HIGH AND RISING
3RD TONE GREEN: LOW AND DIPPING
4TH TONE BLUE: HIGH AND FALLING

high

low

The neutral, unstressed tone is left black. Each entry contains important information about the character's tone and meaning. The page is printed in the character's assigned color, and a graphical representation of the tone's contour is in the upper right corner.

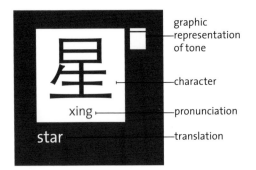

星

xing

star

graphic representation of tone

character

pronunciation

translation

With practice, the synesthetic association between character, tone and color will become stronger and stronger, thus improving both your reading and speaking of Mandarin.

6

The CDs included with this book contain audio tracks with the example sentences from the explanations of the characters. A track listing is included on pg. 241 so that you can read along with the audio, or you can listen and repeat. Male and female voices alternate to provide accurate tonal models.

In addition to this audio (which can be played on any CD player) the second CD contains all of the audio as mp3s with color images of the character discussed. These images are viewable on Apple's iTunes program and on most iPods. Simply insert the second CD into your computer and import the tracks into iTunes. You can now practice with Tone and Color on the go!

Hanyu Pinyin is the official system recognized by the Chinese government for phonetically transcribing the syllables of modern Chinese using the Roman alphabet. The following guidelines are rough approximations, but will assist you in properly reading Pinyin.

a	the *a* in f*a*ther
b	same as English
c	the *ts* in ca*ts*
ch	the *ch* in *ch*urch with tongue curled upward
f/g/h	same as English
i	the *ee* in s*ee*. When preceded by a c, s, or z, *i* is pronounced similar to the *u* in p*u*t. When preceded by a ch, sh, zh, or r, *i* is pronounced like the *ir* sound in sh*ir*t.
j	the *j* in jeep, with the tip of the tongue touching the bottom of the front teeth
k/l/m/n	same as English
o	the *o* in f*o*r

p	same as English
q	the *ch* in *ch*eap with the tongue touching the bottom of the front teeth
s	same as English
sh	the *sh* in *sh*irt, with the tongue curled upward
t	same as English
u	the *ue* in h*ue*. When following a j, q, x, or y, *u* is pronounced like an ü.
ü	the French *u*, an *ee* sound made with the lips pursed forward
x	the *sh* in *sh*e with the tip of the tongue touching the bottom of the front teeth
y	same as English
z	the *ds* in ki*ds*
zh	the *ge* in pur*ge*, with the tongue curled upward

我

wo

I/me

One way to categorize the more than 6,000 languages existing in the world is by word order. While a slight majority of languages use a subject-object-verb (sov) order, English sentences are generally constructed using the order of subject-verb-object (svo):

SUBJECT	VERB	OBJECT
I	study	Chinese.

Luckily for us, Chinese follows a sentence structure very similar to English, allowing for a direct replacement of vocabulary items with little rearrangement of word order.

SUBJECT	VERB	OBJECT
I	study	Chinese.
我	学 xue	中文。 zhong wen

There is also no subject/object distinction between *I*/*me*, *he*/*him*, and *we*/*us*.

他 gei 我...   He gave me...
ta

我 gei 他...   I gave him...
     ta

shi

to be

We have some great news for anyone who's ever studied a Romance language: Chinese verbs do not inflect for number, person or tense. This means that there are no conjugation charts to memorize and no complicated endings to distinguish between *you* (singular) and *you* (plural).

Once you learn a verb, you can use it for all types of subjects. For example:

我是中国人。 zhong guo ren	I am Chinese.
他是中国人。 ta	He is Chinese.
她们是中国人。 ta men	They (fem.) are Chinese.

是 usually links two noun phrases that are equated with each other.

他是yisheng。	He is a doctor.

是 may be omitted when the second noun phrase is a number that refers to age, time or money.

我二十九岁。 er shi jiu sui	I am 29 years old.

ni

you

Like many languages, Chinese has more than one word for *you* when addressing another person, depending on context and social status.

In this book, we will usually use the more informal form of address in Chinese, 你. Please note the change in tone and final sound when switching to the more formal 您 *nin* (pg. 210), and notice that the two characters are very similar except for the addition of the character for heart 心 *xin* (pg. 154) on the bottom.

你的 *de*	your
你们 *men*	you (pl.)
你好 *hao*	hello! (lit., *you good*)
您好	hello! (formal)

Although the informal plural of *you* is 你们 *nimen* (pg. 30), 您们 is unusual. When addressing more than one person in a respectful fashion, it is common to use 大家 *dajia* or 你们大家 (pg. 156).

While gender remains undifferentiated in spoken Mandarin (see 他/她 *ta* on pg. 28), a written feminine counterpart to 你 exists, with the substitution of the character for *woman* 女 *nü* (pg. 128). 妳 is rare in everyday writing, appearing more often in song lyrics and other poetic contexts.

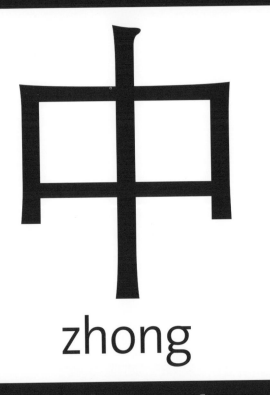

zhong

middle/China

Ideographs (also called ideograms) are characters that define abstract concepts through the use of symbols. 中 is composed of a vertical line bisecting an enclosure to convey the idea of *middle*.

中学 xue	middle school
中饭 fan	lunch
中wu	noon/midday
中年人 nian ren	middle-aged person

Though 中 is used literally to indicate location or order, it is also commonly used in reference to China, the "middle kingdom."

中文 wen	Chinese language
中can	Chinese food
中yi	traditional Chinese medicine

中 can also be used with the preposition 在 *zai* (pg. 32) in constructions that mean *in the process of*.

在学xi中 zai	in the process of studying
在xiuli中	under repair

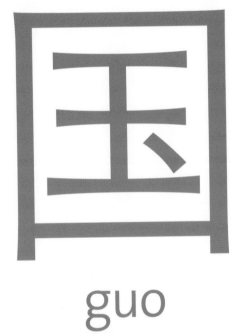

guo

country

While 国 is used in compounds referring to a nation or country in an abstract sense (国家 *guojia state*), it is also used to translate certain names of foreign countries into Chinese. Characters are chosen for their phonetic proximity to the foreign word, which sometimes results in interesting connotations.

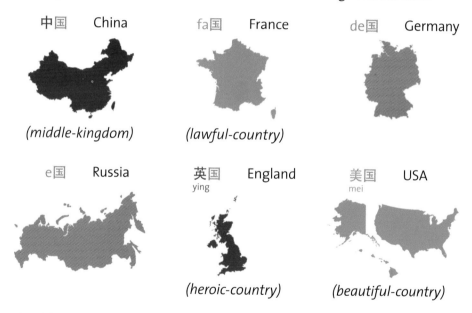

中国 China
(middle-kingdom)

fa国 France
(lawful-country)

de国 Germany

e国 Russia

英国 England
ying
(heroic-country)

美国 USA
mei
(beautiful-country)

It should also be noted that in Taiwan, Mandarin is referred to as 国文 *guowen* or 国语 *guoyu*, literally *national language*.

mei

beauty/USA

美 is composed of the characters for *sheep* 羊 and *big* 大 *da* to suggest a big sheep, something tasty and beautiful in China thousands of years ago.

美li	beautiful
美人	beautiful person
美shu	fine arts

America is phonetically transcribed in hanzi as 美lijian. Modern Chinese uses the abbreviated word 美国 for the United States as well as the following compounds:

bei美zhou	North America
nan美zhou	South America
美jin/美yuan	US dollar

英 *ying* (pg. 35) is another example of using hanzi to phonetically transcribe a foreign word.

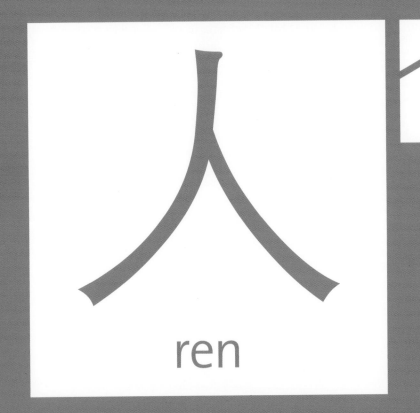

ren

person

Many of the older characters in Chinese were derived from representational drawings created thousands of years ago. 人 is the first character in this book that falls into this category.

Many of these characters have been found on oracle shells that date back as far as the 14th century BC. Though the characters became more stylized and abstracted over the years, most still retain enough of their pictographic elements to be recognized by the beginning reader.

人口 kou	population
美国人	American person
中国人	Chinese person
英国人 ying	English person
han国人	Korean person

ma

question particle

Words that have grammatical meaning but no lexical meaning are called particles. English does not use particles, but many Asian languages use them to indicate questions, suggestions and subject/object relationships. Particles in Chinese are pronounced in a neutral, unstressed tone and usually contain the character for mouth, 口 *kou*.

Forming yes-or-no questions in Chinese couldn't be easier. You simply add the particle 吗 to the end of a declarative sentence.

你是中国人。	You are Chinese.
你是中国人吗?	Are you Chinese?
好吃。 hao chi	It's tasty.
好吃吗?	Is it tasty?

呢 *ne* (pg. 34) is another particle that is extremely useful to the beginning learner. 呢 is used to duplicate a previously asked question, similar to the implication of *and you?* in English.

你好吗?	How are you?
好, 你呢?	Good, and you?

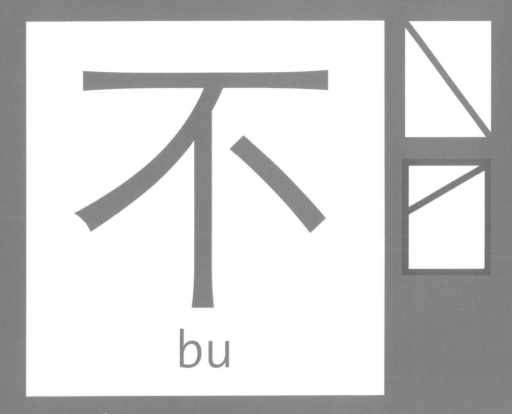

bu

not

Negatives in Chinese are quite simple. A verb or an adjective can be negated simply by placing 不 in front of it (also see 没 *mei*, pg. 72).

他是中国人。　　He is Chinese.
　ta

我不是中国人。　I am not Chinese.

不 is one of the few characters that has more than one pronunciation. It is usually pronounced in the fourth, falling tone.

我不学。　　I don't study.

However, when it is followed by another fourth tone, 不 changes to a second tone syllable.

你不是中国人。　　You are not Chinese.

The construction for *is not*, 不是 *bushi*, is so common that it is useful to memorize this tone combination as a single unit.

我不是学生。　　I am not a student.
　　　xue sheng

Also see 不对 *budui* (pg. 162), 不在 *buzai* (pg. 32) and 不会 *buhui* (pg. 158) for more examples of this tone change.

他
她

ta

he/she

Third person pronouns in Chinese are quite simple. There is only one word for both *he* and *she*, ta. However, while the word is pronounced the same regardless of the person's gender, there are two different written characters denoting male and female. They are introduced here at the same time because of this similarity.

他不是美国人。　　He's not American.

她是中国人吗?　　Is she Chinese?

他是不是英国人?　　Is he English?

ying

Note that the character for *she* differs only in the replacement of the radical on the left with the character for *woman*, 女 *nü* (pg. 128). The female pronoun is a relatively recent addition to the written language.

While not as common as it is in English, 它 *ta* is the gender-neutral pronoun for animals and objects.

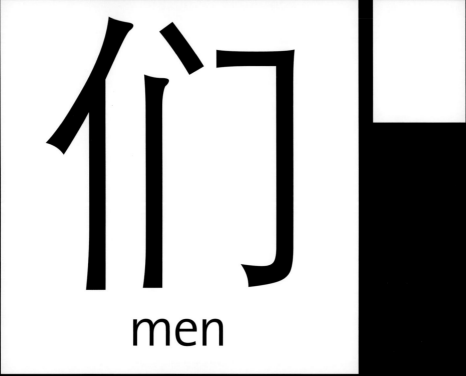

men

PLURALS

Plurals in Chinese are usually dependent on context and situation. There is no equivalent to the *s* in English to indicate whether there is one or more of a given object. There is, however, a particle (always unstressed in speech) to indicate plurality with pronouns and certain other human nouns:

我	I	我们	we
你	you	你们	you (pl.)
他	he	他们	they (masc.)
她	she	她们	they (fem.)
学生 xue sheng	student	学生们	students

Note the following situations in which 们 *cannot* be used:

1. When there is a specific number stated: 四个学生 *sigexuesheng*, not *四个学生们 for *four students*.

2. When the noun is not a person: *书们 does not mean *books*. In Chinese, context alone determines whether 书 means *book* or *books*.

zai

to exist

There is more than one way to indicate existence in Chinese. 在 is the most common verb for speaking about existence in terms of location, as in "he *is in* the house." A location is not necessary when using 在.

他在吗?	Is he in? *(on the phone)*
对**不起**, 他不在。 dui bu qi	I'm sorry, he's not in.

When a location is used, it is placed directly after the verb.

他在中国。	He is in China.
他不在中国。	He is not in China.
你**们**在家吗? jia	Are you (pl.) in the house?

在 can be used as a preposition (see pg. 125) and as an adverb. When combined with other verbs, it indicates actions occurring at the moment (similar to the English *-ing*).

我在**喝**cha。 he	I am drinking tea.
他在吃饭。 chi fan	He is eating.
你在做什么? zuo shen me	What are you doing?

The particle 呢 *ne* (pg. 34) can be optionally added to the end of such progressive sentences, and 没有 *meiyou* (pg. 73) rather than 不 is used to negate them.

ne

ying

England/heroic

Because of the absence of conjugation in Chinese verbs, we can use the dozen or so words we have learned so far to build over 200 well-formed sentences!

Translate the following into Chinese:

Are you Chinese?

....

We are not American.

....

Are they in China?

....

You (pl.) are not Chinese.

....

I'm English. How about you?

....

TONE ASSIGNMENT 1

Write the following characters in their correct tone color.
Hint: one of the characters has two possible tones.

人 中 国 我 不 在 美 你 是 他 她

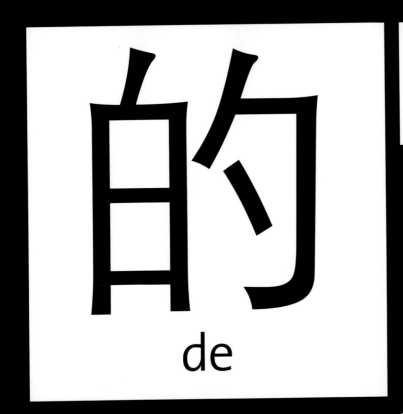

的

de

possessive particle

Because of its many grammatical functions, 的 is the most commonly used character in the Chinese language. As a particle it is always pronounced in the neutral tone.

POSSESSIVE ADJECTIVES AND PRONOUNS

的 is used after a pronoun in much the same way as *s* is used in English to indicate possession:

我的	my/mine
你的	your/yours
他的/她的	his/hers
我们的	our/ours
你们的	your/yours (pl.)
他们的/她们的	their (fem. and masc.)
我的书 shu	my book
你的gou	your dog

的 is often omitted when it defines a close relationship. 我的mama literally means *my mother,* but 我mama is far more common. Certain affiliations are abbreviated in a similar fashion:

我们学xiao xue	our school
他们gongsi	their company

lai

to come

As in English, 来 can be used with or without a destination.

我来。她们不来。　I'll come. They won't come.

When used with a specific location, the destination is placed after the verb. A preposition (such as *to* in English) is not needed.

她来中国。　She'll come to China.

来 is also used idiomatically at restaurants when ordering, and as a colloquial verb similar to *get*:

我来lamian。　I'll have ramen.
我来!　I'll get it! *(the door, the phone, etc.)*

cong来 is an adverb that means *never* when it precedes a negated verb.

我cong来不去jiuba。　I never go to bars.
qu

qu

to go

去 is used in the same way as 来 to indicate simple motion away from the speaker:

我们去美国。 We're going to the United States.

Both 去 and 来 form directional complements when combined with other verbs, depending on the direction of movement relative to the speaker:

jin去	to go in (movement away from the speaker)
jin来	to come in (movement towards the speaker)
上去/下去 shang xia	to go up/to go down
上来/下来	to come up/to come down

Both 去 and 来 have several more uses when combined with other verbs, but these are beyond the scope of this book. 去, when combined with the character for year, means *last year* (lit., *the year that went*):

去年我去了英国。 Last year I went to England.
nian   le

chi

to eat

The character on the left is the radical for *mouth* 口, while the character on the right 乞 shows a man kneeling to beg for something to eat.

吃 is used transitively just as it is in English, with the object following the verb. When placed after a country's name, the addition of the character for *vegetable*, 菜 *cai* (pg. 126), signifies the cuisine of that country.

我不吃中国菜。	I don't eat Chinese food.
这个怎么吃? zhe ge zen me	How is this eaten?

吃bao means *to eat one's fill*.

你吃bao了吗? le	Are you full?

Have you eaten? is often used as a casual greeting in lieu of 你好 *nihao* (pg. 53):

A: 吃过了吗? guo	Have you eaten?
B: 吃过了。你呢?	Yes, how about you?
A: 没有吃。 mei you	Not yet.

he

to drink

喝 is similar to 吃 in tone and composition—the radical 口 again indicating an action with the mouth. For the image on the right, imagine a *person* 人 trapped in an enclosure under the hot *sun* 日 *ri*. All he can think of is a drink.

Here are some common words for drinks in Chinese. Some are phonetic approximations of the English word.

shui	water
kafei	coffee
cha	tea
pijiu	beer
niunai	milk
putaojiu	wine

你喝kafei吗?　　Do you drink coffee?

我不喝kafei。　　I don't drink coffee.

我喝cha。　　I drink tea.

hen

very

English uses the verb *to be* to describe nouns with adjectives: He *is* tall; We *are* hungry. Although we have learned the equational verb 是 which in many ways corresponds to *to be*, this verb is not normally used with adjectival predicates. Instead, a "degree adverb" is placed in between the noun and the adjective. 很 is the most common adverb for this purpose:

	CORRECT	INCORRECT
I am tired.	我很lei。	*我是lei。
She is pretty.	她很piaoliang。	*她是piaoliang。
I am very busy.	我们很mang。	*我们是mang。

While 很 literally means *very* as a degree adverb, it has little meaning when used in this context. 是 is only used with adjectival predicates in situations where emphasis or contrast is implied.

我是高。
gao

I *am* tall (...but not tall enough to reach the shelf, etc.)

Some other common degree adverbs that can be used in between nouns and adjectives are:

zhen	really
feichang	extremely
bijiao	rather
太 tai	too

Adjective predicates are negated by substituting 不 for the degree adverb:

他很高。 gao	He is tall.
他不高。	He is not tall.

As mentioned on pg. 25, yes-or-no questions in Chinese can be formed by adding 吗 at the end of a declarative sentence. As an alternative to using 吗, Chinese has a common construction called *verb-不-verb*. A verb (or an adjective) and its negative form (高 and 不高, for example) are combined to literally ask *tall not tall?* 不 is pronounced in the neutral tone in this construction.

他高不高?	Is he tall?
你们是不是学生? xue sheng	Are you students?

ADJECTIVES 2

ATTRIBUTIVE ADJECTIVES WITH ONE SYLLABLE

As in English, adjectives in Chinese are placed before the noun they modify. When the adjective has only one syllable, it is placed directly in front of the noun:

hua	flowers	baihua	white flowers
cha	tea	hongcha	red tea
gou	dog(s)	大gou da	big dogs

ATTRIBUTIVE ADJECTIVES WITH MORE THAN ONE SYLLABLE

的 is used with compound adjectives of more than one syllable, or when an adjective is modified by an adverb:

piaoliang的人	a beautiful person
很大的gou	a very big dog

好

hao

good

52

The Chinese word for *good* is used in many different contexts.

GREETINGS

你好。	Hello. (lit., *you good*)
你好吗?	How are you?
大家好。 da jia	Hello everybody.

Note that while the first greeting is rhetorical and can be answered with the same "你好," the second greeting is a yes-or-no question that usually requires a response, such as *I'm good*: 我很好. While 你好 can be used at any time of the day, combining 好 with other words creates greetings for different times of the day:

zao上好 shang	good morning
wan上好	good evening

COMPOUND ADJECTIVES

好 combines with common verbs to form several adjectives:

好吃	delicious (lit., *good to eat*)
好喝	delicious *(for drinks)*
好看 kan	attractive
好听 ting	pleasing to the ear

duo

many/much

多 is a pictograph of two *moons* 月 *yue*, to convey the idea of *many* or *much*. *Many* is an adjective, so it is often used with 很.

他有很多书。　　He has many books.
you　　shu

Human age in Chinese is measured with 多大 *duoda*. Questions about age in Chinese can be answered by simply adding the suffix 岁 *sui* (pg. 218) to your age. As with other number predicates, 是 is not necessary.

你今年多大岁shu?　　How old are you?
jin nian　da

我二十九岁。　　I'm 29 years old.
er shi jiu sui

It should be noted that age is something to be proud of in Chinese culture. Asking someone's age, regardless of gender, is perhaps more common and acceptable than in other societies.

多 can be used as the adverb *more* when it precedes a verb.

你要多说中文。　　You need to speak Chinese more.
yao　shuo　wen

shao

few/little

Take care to not confuse 小 *xiao* (pg. 60) and 少 *shao*. 少 can be used in front of a verb as an adverb meaning *little*.

taiwan很少下xue。   It snows very little in Taiwan.
_{xia}

The antonym pair 多少 is very important for the beginning reader. Meaning *how much* or *how many*, it is used in several different contexts. Most questions that seek a numerical answer use 多少 instead of 什么 *shenme* (pg. 75). For example, instead of asking *what* someone's phone number is, in Chinese you ask *how much*.

你的dian话号ma是多少?   What is your phone number?
_{hua hao}

多少 can be placed in front of common nouns to ask about both countable and non-countable quantities.

多少qian?   How much is it? *(when shopping)*

你会写多少hanzi?   How many hanzi can you write?
_{hui xie}

da

big

The character for *big* is a pictograph depicting a *person* 人 with his arms outstretched. The word has several common idiomatic uses:

大家 jia	everybody (*big-house*)	
大人	adult (*big-person*)	
大yi	coat (*big-clothing*)	
大学 xue	university (*big-study*)	
大sheng	loudly (*big-voice*)	
大gai	probably	

大 also means *old* in reference to human age.

你今年多大岁shu? How old are you?
jin nian   sui

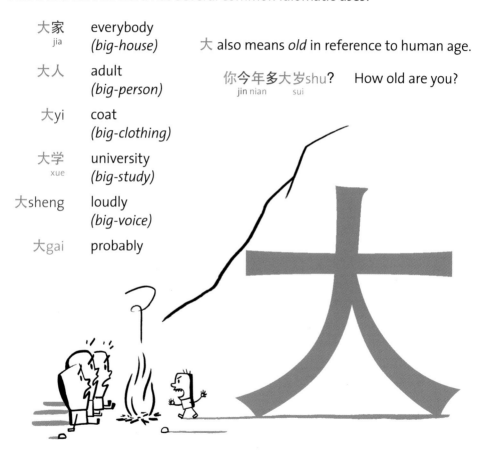

59

xiao

small

小 is an ideogram of *something* 八 split by a vertical line, thus producing a smaller quantity. The word for *small* also has many idiomatic uses:

小吃	snack	*(small-eat)*
小看 kan	belittle, trivialize	*(small-look)*
小心 xin	caution, care	*(small-heart)*
小学 xue	elementary school	*(small-study)*
小时 shi	hour	*(small-time)*

It is also interesting that several abstract nouns in Chinese are formed by combining two antonyms:

大小	size	*(big-small)*
多少	quantity	*(many-few)*
qingzhong	weight	*(light-heavy)*

shu

book

In an effort to increase literacy and eliminate redundancy in the oldest writing system in the world still in use, simplified Chinese characters have been in use in mainland China since the 1950s.

	TRADITIONAL	SIMPLIFIED
book	書	书
to allow	讓	让
medicine	醫	医
several	幾	几
voice	聲	声

Many of these characters were simplified using methods derived from Chinese calligraphy. Strokes that would often be combined when written quickly with a brush were similarly reduced in simplified characters. In other cases, complex characters were merged with simpler characters that had similar sounds. Traditional characters are still used in Taiwan and in many overseas Chinese communities, but the beginning learner of Chinese as a foreign language will certainly appreciate the clarity of the simplified writing system.

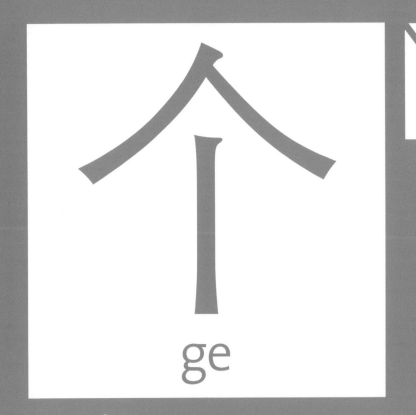

ge

unit

Like certain other Asian languages, Chinese uses measure words (also called classifiers) to count both abstract and concrete nouns. A single number in Chinese cannot represent a quantity without a measure word. While there are dozens of measure words in modern Chinese, 个 is the most common and general. 个 can be substituted when a specific measure word is not known, making it particularly useful for the beginning learner. 个 is often unstressed in speech.

	CORRECT	INCORRECT
five people	五个人 wu	*五人
one month	一个月 yi yue	*一月
six teachers	六个laoshi liu	*六laoshi

个 is also used in some compound nouns meaning *personal* or *individual*.

个人   personal

这是我个人yi见。   This is my personal opinion.
zhe   jian

个zi   stature/build

他的个zi很高。   He is of (a) very tall build.
gao

zhe/zhei

this

DEMONSTRATIVES 1

Chinese only has two demonstratives (*this* and *that*), and they are each used in two ways.

DEMONSTRATIVE PRONOUNS

Both 这 and its counterpart 那 *na* (pg. 68) can be used in place of animate or inanimate objects:

这是我**的**书。	This is my book.
那是我**的**太太。 _{tai tai}	That is my wife.
那是我**的**zhangfu。	That is my husband.

SPECIFIERS

这 and 那 can be used as specifier adjectives when combined with a measure word (pg. 65).

那个人是你**的**laoshi。	That person is your teacher.

这 and 那 are also combined with 么 *me* (pg. 76) to mean *so* or *such*.

你中文说**得**这么好! _{wen shuo de}	You speak Chinese so well!

那

na/nei

that

那么 also functions as an interjection similar to *well* or *in that case* when used at the beginning of a sentence.

明天我有kong。 ming tian you	I have free time tomorrow.
那么，我们一起去ba。 　　　　yi qi	Well why don't we go together?

LOCATION PRONOUNS

When combined with the word 儿 *er* (pg. 130), 这 and 那 form the words *here* and *there*. 儿 is unstressed when used this way, and combines with the preceding word to form a single syllable.

他不在那儿。	He is not there.
这儿有很多人。	There are a lot of people here.

While 这儿 and 那儿 are more common in Beijing and the northern parts of China, southern speakers add 里 *li* (pg. 124) to 这 and 那 to form *here* and *there*:

你们在那里吗?	Are you (pl.) there?
这里可以chouyan吗? ke yi	Can I smoke here?

这 and 那 are often pronounced as zhei and nei with no change in meaning.

you

to have

This character is commonly described as a hand grasping a piece of meat (represented by the character for *moon* 月) to indicate possession. There is an overlap in meaning between the verbs *possess* and *exist* in Chinese. Both verbs can be translated with the word 有.

POSSESSION

有 means *to have* for both animate and inanimate objects.

她有很多书。 She has many books.

我有一个meimei。 I have a younger sister.
　　 yi

EXISTENCE

有 is translated as *exist* when the subject of the sentence is a location, similar to *there is* or *there are* in English. Note that with few exceptions, location always precedes the verb in Chinese.

这儿有很多书。 There are many books here.

有 can also refer to unspecified nouns, similar to the use of *some* in English.

有时 sometimes
shi

有个人 someone

mei

without

While 不 is used to negate most verbs, it cannot be used with 有. 没 is always used to negate 有

> 我有一个gege。 I have an older brother.
>
> 她没有gege。 She doesn't have an older brother.

没 and 没有 are used to indicate that an action didn't occur, or has not yet occurred. 有 is often omitted in speech.

> 我没去过中国。 I haven't been to China. (lit., *I am without the experience of going to China.*)

没 and 没有 are also used in certain verb phrases, such as the negation of actions in the past:

> 他昨天没来。 He didn't come yesterday.
> zuo tian

有没有 can be used to form *yes-or-no* questions, just like *verb*-不-*verb* (pg. 50). The question particle 吗 is not used in this construction.

> 你有没有qian? Do you have money?

shen

what

什 is never used without its counterpart 么 *me* (pg. 76). It is used in content questions, in just the same way as *what* in English. Please note the word order: question words in Chinese (*who, what, where*) are placed in the same location as the answer.

那是什么?	What is that?
你在吃什么?	What are you eating?

什么 is also used directly in front of nouns when asking for information:

你jiao什么mingzi?	What is your name?
	(lit., *You are called what name?*)
那是什么菜?	What dish is that?
cai	

There are also several common expressions that contain 什么:

什么时候 shi hou	when (lit., *what time*)
什么difang	where (lit., *what place*)
什么liyou	for what reason
没什么	It's nothing. (a modest response to 谢谢, *thank you* or 对不起, *sorry*)
xie	dui qi

me

what

么 always combines with another character to form a compound word. It is never used alone. While 什么 (see pg. 75) is used as a question word, it also has many functions as a pronoun similar to *something*:

我想买点儿什么。 I want to buy something.
xiang mai dian er

With the addition of 都 *dou* (pg. 192) or 也 *ye* (pg. 120), it means *everything* or *anything*:

他什么都吃。 He eats everything.
我什么也不zhidao。 I don't know anything.

都 can also be added to the aforementioned compound question nouns.

什么difang都有人。 There are people everywhere.
他什么时候都很高xing。 He is always happy.
shi hou gao

么 also combines with 这 and 那 to form the adverbs 这么 and 那么 (pg. 67).

为

wei

for

为 is a preposition that means *for* or *for the sake of* when pronounced in the fourth tone.

我为你买书。   I'll buy books for you.
mai

为你**的**fangbian   for your convenience

为什么 (lit., *for what*) is used for *why* and is usually placed before the verb:

你为什么不吃?   Why aren't you eating?

他为什么学英文?   Why is he studying English?
xue ying wen

以为 *yiwei*, with 为 pronounced in the second tone, is used idiomatically as a special verb that means *thought erroneously*. It is used when one originally thought something was true but later discovers it to be false.

o, 我以为他在这儿。   Oh, I thought he was here.
er

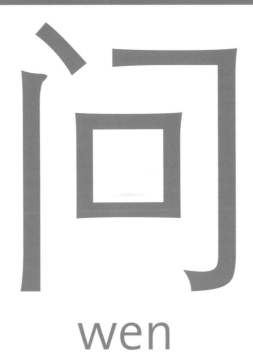

wen

to ask

gao

tall

qing

please

请 is used at the beginning of polite imperatives.

请吃。	Please eat.
请jin, 请jin!	Come in! Come in!

It is also used as a verb meaning *invite* or *ask*,

我请了她吃饭。 fan	I invited her to dinner.
我请你去喝kafei, 好吗?	I'd like to invite you to have coffee with me, okay?

as well as in the set expression 请问 used to get someone's attention (lit., *may I ask?*).

请问, beijingzhan在哪儿? na er	Excuse me, where is Beijing Station?
请问, 您guixing? nin	Excuse me, what is your name? *(formal)*

谢

xie

thanks

谢 is never used alone. It has a similar shape to 请 *please* (pg. 82).

谢谢   Thanks

谢谢你   Thank you

Nouns can be placed directly after 谢谢 to express gratitude for something specific.

谢谢你**的**bangmang。   Thanks for your help.

谢谢你**的**dian话。   Thanks for your phone call.

hua

Chinese has a number of set expressions that are used to say *you're welcome*. Most are essentially modest denials and deflections of thanks.

不谢。   No need to thank me.

不keqi。   No need to be so polite.

没什么。   It's nothing.

哪里 *nali* (pg. 199) is also occasionally used for this purpose, in the same way it is used to deflect praise or compliments.

zai

again

再 can be used as an adverb that means *again*.

请再听一ci。   Please listen again.
　　 ting

再来wan儿。   Please come again. *(to a visitor)*
　　　 er

再 is also used with sequences of actions:

你做好gongke再chu去。   After you finish your homework,
　 zuo   (then) you can go out.

However, the beginning learner is most likely to encounter this character in the Chinese expression for *good-bye*: 再见 *zaijian*.

jian

to see/to meet

见 was originally a pictograph of an exaggerated eye on two legs. It is used as a suffix for certain verbs expressing sensation, such as 看 *kan* (pg. 96) and 听 *ting* (pg. 98), to express perception. A neutral-tone 不 is placed between the verbs to express the inability to perceive something.

我听**不见**。	I can't hear.
我zuijin没看见她。	I haven't seen her lately.

见 also corresponds to the verb *to meet*.

你见**过我的**pengyou吗?	Have you met my friend?
再见。	See you later. (lit., *Meet you later.*)
明天见。 ming tian	See you tomorrow.
下zhou见。 xia	See you next week.

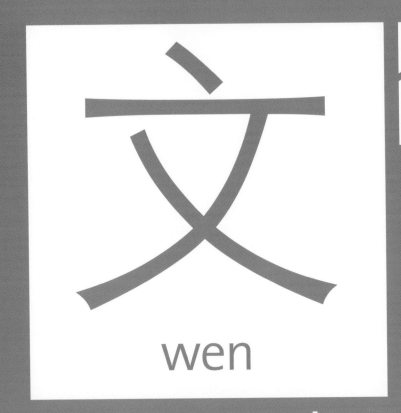

wen

writing/culture

While 文 technically refers to written language, it is sometimes used for the spoken language as well (see pg. 19 for names of countries).

中文	Chinese
英文	English
fa文	French

文 is used in many compounds dealing with scholarship, civilization and culture.

文fa	grammar
文hua	culture
文学	literature
文明 ming	civilization

shuo

to speak

Many useful phrases for the beginning learner involve 说:

你说什么?	What did you say?
请再说一ci。 yi	Please say it again.
你会说中文吗? hui	Can you speak Chinese?
我会说一点儿中文。 dian er	I speak a little Chinese.
你说得很好。 de	You speak very well.
你可以说得man一点儿吗? ke yi de	Could you speak a little slower?

说 also appears in some common compound expressions:

小说	novel
听说 ting	I've heard it said... *as in*
听说你会说中文。	I've heard that you speak Chinese.

Hanzi containing the radical for *speech* (言 simplified as 讠) often have meanings related to speech or language:

请	please (pg. 82)	谢	thanks (pg. 84)
语 yu	language (pg. 203)	话 hua	speech/talk (pg. 204)

xue

to study

Translate the following into Chinese:

Is this your book?

....

Why aren't you coming?

....

He doesn't have anything.

....

I have a lot of books.

....

What are you eating?

....

kan

to look

看 is used to mean *look*, *watch* and *read*.

我不看dianshi。 I don't watch television.

他每天都看bao吗? Does he read the newspaper every
mei tian dou day?

When combined with 要 *yao* (pg. 200), 看 means *it depends* (lit., *one has to see*).

你也去吗? Are you going also?
ye

要看你在不在。 It depends on if you are there or
not.

Many verbs in Chinese become idiomatic expressions meaning *a little* or *a bit* with the addition of an unstressed 一 *yi* (pg. 132).

我看一看。 I'll take a little look.

看 can also mean *consider* or *regard*.

我看他太pang了。 I consider him to be too fat.
tai le

听

ting

to hear

fan

meal/rice

了

le

completion particle

了 is used in a large number of grammatical constructions, though many are beyond the scope of this book. A few that are useful to the beginning learner are:

1. 了 is used to show that a verb has been completed. This is different from tense, which in Chinese is indicated by time expressions.

我吃了。	I ate/have eaten.
他们来了。	They have come.
你吃过了吗? guo	Have you eaten? (often used as a casual greeting instead of 你好)

2. 了 appears in certain adjectival expressions, the most common of which is 太 *tai* ...了, which means *very* or *too*.

太gui了。	It's too expensive
太好了!	Great! (lit., *too good!*)

3. 了 is also used at the end of a sentence to indicate a change in state.

现在几点了? ji dian	What time is it now?
我jiehun了。	I'm married now.

tai

too

Take care to not confuse 大 and 太. The beginning learner is most likely to encounter 太 combined with 了 in superlative expressions such as *too expensive* 太gui了, *too good* 太好了, and *too much* 太多了. Negation of this construction is possible, such as in 不太好 *not too good*.

太太 means *wife*, and is also a title similar to *Mrs.* in English.

请问, 李太太在吗?　　Excuse me, is Mrs. Li in?
　　　li

李 is the most common surname in the world, even when discounting its Korean and Vietnamese derivations. Over 100 million people in China (more than three times the population of Canada) are named 李. 王 *wang*, 陈 *chen*, 张 *zhang*, and 刘 *liu* are also extremely common surnames.

Titles such as 太太 always follow the surname in Chinese, and professional titles such as laoshi *teacher* and shifu *master/tradesman* are more commonly used in Chinese than in English.

王xian生 sheng	Mr. Wang
陈小jie	Miss Chen
张laoshi	Teacher Zhang
刘shifu	Master Worker Liu

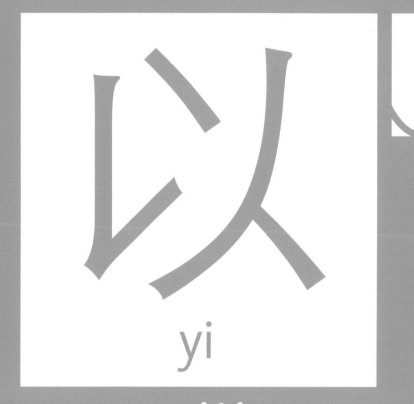

yi

preposition

以 combines with several characters to form common adverbs:

以前 qian	before, prior to
以后 hou	after, later
以上 shang	above
以下 xia	below
以nei	inside, within
以wai	outside, beyond

Since verbs do not inflect for tense in Chinese, these adverbs of time are extremely important for establishing when something happens. Adverbs such as *before*, *after* and *later* generally precede the verb and sometimes the subject as well.

他以前在中国zhu过三年。 guo san nian	He lived in China for three years.
三年以后我去美国。	I went to the US three years later.

以前 and 以后 can also specify the sequence in which events take place.

我们吃了饭以后, jiu去你的家。 jia	After we eat, we'll go to your house.
我吃zao饭以前xizao。	Before I eat breakfast, I take a bath.

qian

before/front

hou

after/back

xian

to appear/present

This character combines *king* 王 *wang* with *watch* 见 . When the king appears, everyone is watching. 现 combines with 在 to form the expression *now*. As with other time adverbs, 现在 needs to precede the verb.

我现在学中文。	I am studying Chinese now.
现在几点?	What time is it (now)?
ji dian	

现 combines with jin, *gold*, for *cash* (lit., *ready money*) and other compound nouns that refer to the present time.

你可以gei我现jin吗?	Can you pay in cash?
ke	
现dai	modern/contemporary
biao现	behavior
现shi	reality

dian

point

点 originally meant *point* or *dot*. The traditional form conveyed the *black* 黑 marks left by a *fire*: 點. In addition to this original meaning, it now has several other idiomatic uses. When telling time, 点 is used as the unit for hours. The verb 是 is optional.

现在(是)两点。　It's two o'clock.
    liang

While 点 is used for clock time, it should be noted that 小时 *xiaoshi* (pg. 61) is used for counting individual hours, and therefore requires a measure word.

三点　　three o'clock
san

三个小时　　three hours

点 is also used with 一 *yi* (pg. 132) to mean *a little* or *a bit*. Note that in Beijing and northern parts of China, 儿 *er* (pg. 130) is added to the end of this word.

一点儿cha　　a little tea

点 is sometimes repeated to emphasize *little*.

你会说中文吗?　　Can you speak Chinese?
  hui

一点点。　　Only a little.

ban

half

半 is a pictograph of something being divided in *half* down the middle. 半 is commonly used in time expressions. With clock time, 半 is used to express "half past the hour."

现在七点半。　　It's 7:30.
　　　qi

Since 半 is used as a number, it requires a measure word. When combined with the measure word 个, 半 is used to represent a *half* for both common and abstract nouns.

半个小时　　half an hour
　　shi

半个月　　half a month
　　yue

半个pingguo　　half an apple

If the expression refers to a quantity greater than one (*two and a half*, etc.), 半 needs to follow the measure word in the order *number + measure word + 半*. Its usage above for clock time also conforms to this rule. In Chinese, *3:30* is 三点半 *sandianban* (lit., *three and a half dots on the clock*).

一个半pingguo　　one and a half apples
yi

三bei半kafei　　three and a half cups of coffee

四个半小时　　four and a half hours
si

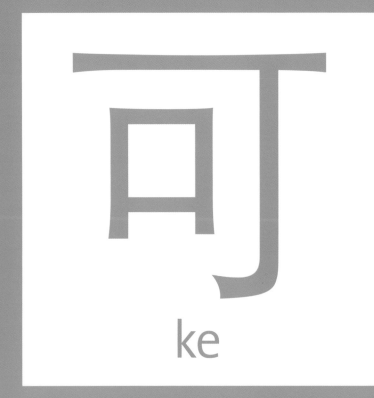

ke

may/can

可以 is a common expression meaning *can*, *may* or *could* in polite questions and requests. As with *can* in English, 可以 is used in sentences that refer to ability as well as sentences that refer to permissibility.

我现在可以chu去吗?	May I go out now?
你可以写你的mingzi吗? xie	Could you write your name?
她今年十七岁。不可以喝pijiu。 jin nian shi qi sui	She's 17 years old. She can't drink beer.

可 is also part of several other common words.

可neng	possible, maybe
可是	but, however
可ai	cute (lit., *lovable*)
可xiao	funny (lit., *laughable*)
可pa	frightful, scary

Coca-Cola has been phonetically translated as 可口可乐 *kekoukele*. Literally, *can please the mouth*.

还可以 *haikeyi* is an understated (sometimes modest) way to say *not bad*.

那budianying怎么样? zen yang	How was the movie?
还可以。	Not bad.

shi

time

The full form of 时 showed the *sun* 日 rising next to a *temple* 寺 (the place where time was kept). The character is used in many compound words that deal with time.

时**候**
hou

time
(as a general abstract concept)

时**间**
jian

time (as a more specific, measurable concept)

时dai

age, era

时**期**
qi

period

什么时**候**

when

hou

time/climate

While 候 is used as a verb meaning *to wait*, it is also a component of two common nouns:

TIME

In most parts of mainland China, 候 in 时候 is pronounced in the unstressed, neutral tone.

我有时**候**去她**的**家。

jia

Sometimes I go to her house. (lit., *There are times when I go to her house.*)

你什么时**候**来？

When are you coming?

Note when *time* is used as a measurable noun, 时间 *shijian* is used instead.

我没有时**间**。

I don't have time.

CLIMATE

中国**的**qi候怎么样？

zen yang

How's the climate in China?

ye

also

Chinese does not make a distinction between *also* and *either*. 也 is used for both positive and negative sentences. 也 is always placed before the verb.

他是美国人。	He is American.
他的太太也是美国人。	His wife is American also.
他不是中国人。	He is not Chinese.
他的太太也不是中国人。	His wife is not Chinese either.

也 is also placed after question words to emphasize words such as *anything*, *nothing* and *nowhere*.

我什么也看不见。	I can't see anything.
我mama什么也不吃。	My mother isn't eating anything.

Notice that 也 is the right-hand side of both *he* 他 and *she* 她 (pg. 28).

suo

place

所 is used in many compound words for places.

ce所	bathroom
zhen所	clinic
paichu所	police station

It is also used as a measure word for certain buildings, houses and schools.

两所学xiao	two schools
liang	

所 is also part of some common words.

所以	so, therefore
所有	all

li

inside

在 is combined with 里 to form prepositions that mean *inside*. The word or phrase indicating location is placed between these two words.

在家里   inside the house
　jia

在hai里   in the sea

里 is an ancient unit of length equal to about half a *kilometer* gong里, or about a third of a *mile* 英里.

一gong里   one kilometer
yi

Please see pg. 69 for more information about how 里 combines with demonstratives to form *here* and *there*.

cai

vegetable/dish

nan

man

nü

woman

The Chinese characters for *male* and *female* are both derived from early pictographs. 男 depicts a *field* 田 and the character for *strength* 力 to imply that *men* provided strength in the fields. 女 is a pictograph of a *woman* sitting or kneeling.

男人	man
女人	woman
男haizi/男hai儿er	boy
女haizi/女hai儿	girl
男pengyou	boyfriend
女pengyou	girlfriend

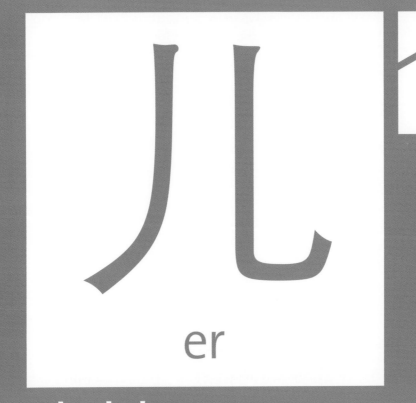

er

child/son

儿 was originally a pictograph depicting a child with two legs and a large head: 兒. Sadly, character simplification has left only the legs. 儿 is used when talking about children. 儿zi is *son* in Chinese, and the addition of the character for *woman* 女 (pg. 128) makes the word 女儿 *daughter*.

我有一个儿zi。	I have a son.
他没有女儿。	He doesn't have a daughter.

While few words in standard Mandarin end with an *r* sound, a large number of words are suffixed with 儿 with no change in meaning. The final consonant of the original character, if present, is replaced with an *r* to make a single, fluid syllable. The tone of the preceding character is maintained, essentially deleting the tone of 儿. This linguistic trend originated in the Beijing area, but has since spread to other parts of the country. It is important for the beginning learner to read these two characters as just one syllable.

ge/ge儿	song
hua/hua儿	flower
一点/一点儿	a little
yi	

See pages 69 and 199 for more information on how 儿 combines with 那, 这 and 哪 *na*.

一

yi

one

132

Like 不, 一 has simple tone changing rules that the beginning student should keep in mind.

1. 一 is pronounced in the fourth tone before words in the first, second or third tone.

我会说一点儿。   I can speak a little.
　　　hui

2. 一 is pronounced in the second tone before words in the fourth tone.

他有一个meimei。   He has one little sister.

3. 一 is pronounced in the first tone when pronounced in isolation or when counting.

一, 二, 三...   1, 2, 3...
　　er san

一 is also often pronounced *yao* when giving phone numbers to avoid confusion with 七 *qi* (pg. 139).

我的dian话号ma是   My phone number is 6341-5871.
　　hua hao
六三四一五八七一。
liu san si yao wu ba

er

two

三

san

three

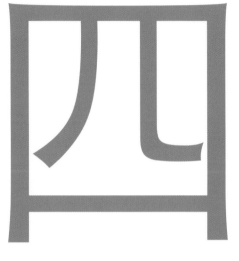

si

four

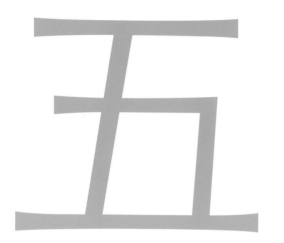

wu

five

liu

six

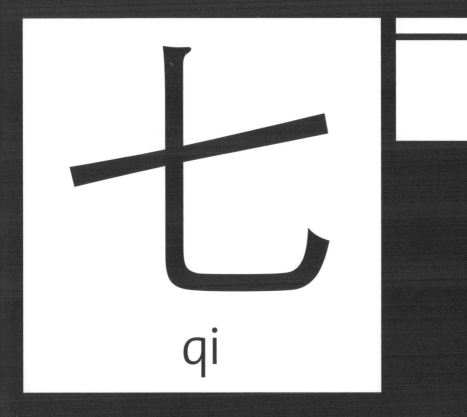

qi

seven

139

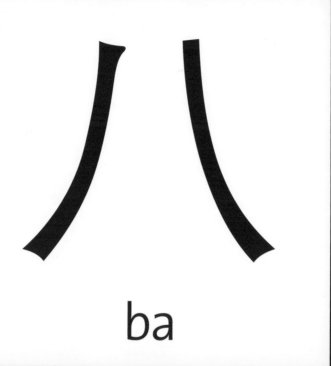

ba

eight

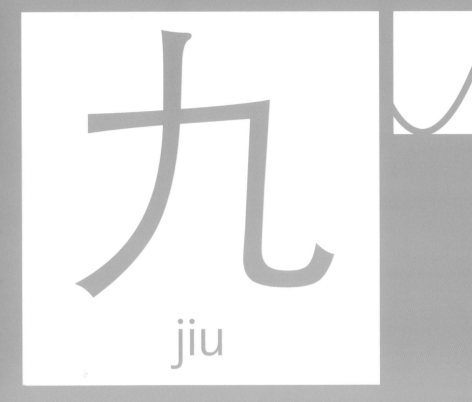

九

jiu

nine

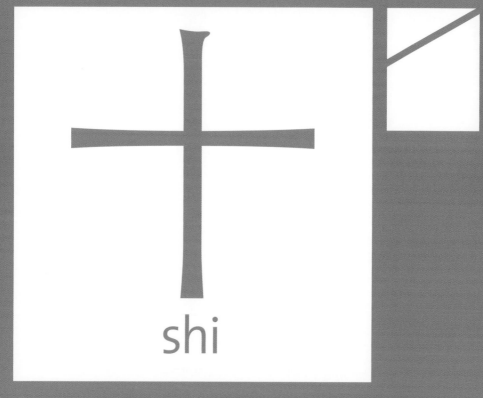

shi

ten

The numbers 1–99 can be expressed in Chinese using only 10 individual words (compared to 27 in English). Composing the numbers 11–99 in Chinese is merely a matter of placing the units digit after the tens digit (much like writing numbers using Arabic numerals).

十七=17
ten + seven units

二十八=28
two tens + eight units

六十=60
six tens + zero units

Numbers larger than 99 follow the same pattern, using the following units (365=三百六十五):

百 100
bai

千 1,000
qian

万 10,000
wan

Particular care must be taken when a number contains a zero. 零 *ling zero* (often a more circular Arabic zero ◯ in casual communication) must be added to fill any non-final empty decimal place.

四百◯九   409 (◯ fills the tens place)
三千◯四十   3,040 (◯ fills the hundreds place)

liang

two

TWO KINDS OF *TWO*

Chinese has two words for *two*. 二 is used for mathematics and for compound numbers such as 二十 *twenty*, and for compound nouns such as *Tuesday* (星期二 *xingqier* pg. 149) and *February* (二月 *eryue* pg. 173). For counting objects and telling time (which is essentially "counted" in Chinese: 三点 refers to counting three dots on a clock), 两 is used.

	CORRECT	INCORRECT
two people	两个人	*二个人
two o'clock	两点	*二点

现在两点半。 It's 2:30.

他今年两岁。 He's two years old this year.
jin nian   sui

我有两个jiejie。 I have two older sisters.

星

xing

star

星 is a character that combines *sun* 日 *ri* and *birth* 生 *sheng* to indicate a source of light. When used as a common noun, 星 is often doubled:

天上有很多星星。　There are many stars in the sky.
tian shang

星 is combined with 期 *qi* (pg. 148) to form the word *week*, as in the following expressions:

上个星期　last week

下个星期　next week
xia

In a literal borrowing from English, in Chinese a celebrity is also called a *star*.

他是有ming的ming星。　He is a famous celebrity.

期

qi

period

Chinese counts the days of the week rather than naming them,

M	T	W	Th	F	Sa
星期一	星期二	星期三	星期四	星期五	星期六

with the exception of

星期天/星期日   Sunday
tian   ri

Weeks are counted using the measure word 个.

两个星期   two weeks

期 is also used in compound nouns that refer to a period of time.

学期   semester (lit., *study period*)

期间   period of time
jian

Translate the following into Chinese:

What day is it today?

⋯⋯⋯⋯⋯⋯⋯⋯⋯⋯⋯⋯⋯⋯⋯⋯⋯⋯⋯⋯⋯⋯⋯⋯⋯⋯⋯⋯⋯⋯⋯⋯⋯⋯⋯

Today is Wednesday.

⋯⋯⋯⋯⋯⋯⋯⋯⋯⋯⋯⋯⋯⋯⋯⋯⋯⋯⋯⋯⋯⋯⋯⋯⋯⋯⋯⋯⋯⋯⋯⋯⋯⋯⋯

What time is it now?

⋯⋯⋯⋯⋯⋯⋯⋯⋯⋯⋯⋯⋯⋯⋯⋯⋯⋯⋯⋯⋯⋯⋯⋯⋯⋯⋯⋯⋯⋯⋯⋯⋯⋯⋯

It's 11:30 now.

⋯⋯⋯⋯⋯⋯⋯⋯⋯⋯⋯⋯⋯⋯⋯⋯⋯⋯⋯⋯⋯⋯⋯⋯⋯⋯⋯⋯⋯⋯⋯⋯⋯⋯⋯

He doesn't eat Chinese food either.

⋯⋯⋯⋯⋯⋯⋯⋯⋯⋯⋯⋯⋯⋯⋯⋯⋯⋯⋯⋯⋯⋯⋯⋯⋯⋯⋯⋯⋯⋯⋯⋯⋯⋯⋯

Are you English also?

⋯⋯⋯⋯⋯⋯⋯⋯⋯⋯⋯⋯⋯⋯⋯⋯⋯⋯⋯⋯⋯⋯⋯⋯⋯⋯⋯⋯⋯⋯⋯⋯⋯⋯⋯

TONE ASSIGNMENT 2

Write the following characters in their correct tone color.

也 时 半 五 说 学 有 没 喝 看 吃 四

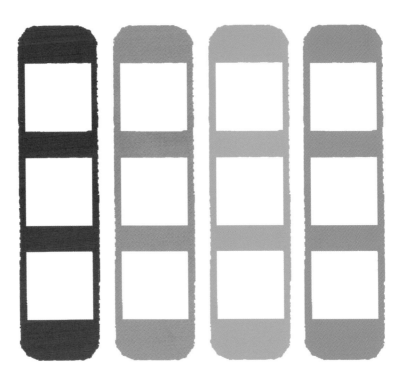

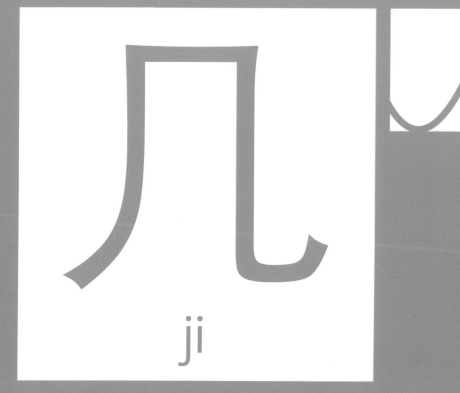

ji

how many

几 is a question word for asking about numbers, *how many*, or an adjective meaning *several* or *a few*. In either case, its usage is limited to relatively small numbers such as hours (pg. 111) or days of the month (pg. 173). It is always followed by a classifier.

你**的生日是**几月几**号?**
sheng ri   yue   hao

When is your birthday? (lit., *Your birthday is what month and what day?*)

现在几**点?**

What time is it now?

今天星期几**?**
jin tian

What day is it today?

Because 几 is limited to small quantities, it may be used for asking the age of children, but not of adults.

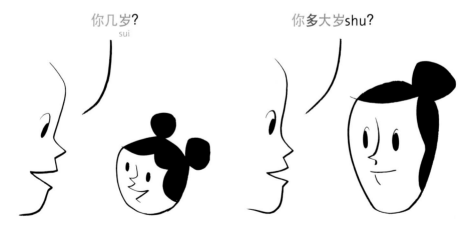

你几岁?
sui

你多大岁shu?

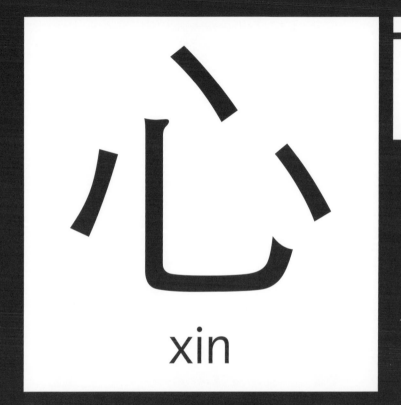

xin

heart

xie

to write

jia

home

家 is a pictograph of a *pig* 豕 under (or perhaps outside) a roof or a house. Many years ago, the house was the building where you would keep such a domesticated animal.

家 sometimes blurs the distinction between *house* and *family*, as in the following exchange:

你家有几口人?* How many people are in your family?
kou

我家有五口人。 There are five people in my family.

Notice that the possessive particle 的 is often omitted in regard to close relationships (such as family members or friends).

家 is also used as a measure word for certain commercial buildings, and as a part of compound nouns denoting certain specialists or experts:

shu学家 mathematician
(number-study-specialist)

ke学家 scientist
(science-study-specialist)

zuo家 writer
(create-specialist)

*While 个 is the usual classifier for people, 口 is used when counting family members (lit., *mouths to feed*).

hui

to be able

会 can be used in front of a verb to express ability.

你会说中文吗?　　Can you speak Chinese?

我会说一点儿。　　I can speak a little.

会 can also imply possibility in the future.

他明天会去。　　He may go tomorrow.
　ming tian

会 also means *meet*, as in the following words:

会yi　　meeting

会见　　to meet (formal)

会chang　　meeting place/conference room

kai会　　to hold a meeting

会 is also placed at the end of certain verbs to form words signifying different kinds of meetings or competitions.

yundong会　　athletic competition
　　　　　　　(exercise-meet)

yinyue会　　concert
　　　　　　(music-meet)

nian

year

qi

to rise

dui

correct

对 is often used as a one-word response to show agreement, much like the English word *yes*. However, the beginning learner should note that in Chinese it is more common to answer a *yes-or-no* question affirmatively with a verb. This efficient form of response, where the subject is dropped and a sentence is composed of only one verb, is an elegant feature of Chinese.

你下个月去吗? xia yue	Are you going next month?
去。	Yes.
他有我的书吗?	Does he have my book?
有。	Yes.

对 means *opposite* or *towards* in certain compound expressions.

对话 hua	conversation
对不起。	Excuse me/I'm sorry.

In an abstract sense, 对 also means *to* or *towards* a person.

他对我很keqi。	He is very polite towards me.
谢谢你对我这么好。	Thank you for being so good to me.

样

yang

style

样 means *kind*, *type* or *sort*. In addition to the commonly used expression 怎么样 *zenmeyang* (pg. 167), it is also used in the word for *same*, 一样 (lit., *one type*).

这是一样**的吗?**	Is this the same?
不, 那是不一样**的。**	No, that's different.

The meaning of *type* is extended to *style* or *manner* in the following compounds.

样shi	style
样zi	form, appearance
这样	like this/this way
那样	like that/that way

这样 and 那样 are used for *this way* and *that way* respectively.

我这样做。 zuo	I do it this way.
这个怎么吃?	How is this eaten?
这样吃。	You eat it this way.

zen

how

怎 is never used alone. It is often found with 么 to form a compound similar to the English *how*. Place 怎么 in front of a verb to ask about means or methods.

中文怎么说?   How do you say (it) in Chinese?

你怎么去?   How are you going?

When 了 is added at the end, you can form the expression *what's wrong?* or *what happened?*

你怎么了?   What's wrong with you?

怎么样 is frequently used for *how is it?* or *what's it like?*

美国的天qi怎么样?   What's the weather like in the USA?
tian

zuijin怎么样?   How've you been lately?

怎么样 is sometimes shortened to 怎样, especially in writing, and when placed in front of a noun also means *what kind of*.

得

de

verb particle

得 is a particle used to introduce a complement to a verb in Chinese. When pronounced *de* in the neutral tone and placed after a verb, it may be followed by an adjective to describe an action. Take care to not confuse this with the particle 的, which is pronounced identically.

他吃得很man。　　He eats very slowly.

你英文说得很好。　　You speak English well.

不 is placed after 得 when using a negated adjective.

他写得不好。　　He doesn't write well.
　　　　　　　　　(lit., *He writes not well.*)

Pronounced *dei* in the third tone and placed before the verb, 得 means *must* or *have to*.

我现在得吃饭了。　　I have to eat now.

得 also means *require*, as in

买那ben书得多少qian?　　How much money do I need to buy
mai　　　　　　　　　　　that book?

得

dei

must

jian

period

yue

month/moon

As with days of the week, Chinese months are numbered rather than named. This makes it possible to learn how to say all 365 days of the year within seconds provided you know how to count in Chinese.

Days of the month, with the suffix 号 *hao* (pg. 174) or 日 *ri* (pg. 180) appended after the number, follow the month as in English.

一月十四 (号／日)	January 14th
九月二 (号／日)	September 2nd
十二月二十八 (号／日)	December 28th

Note that the year precedes the month in Chinese dates (going from largest to smallest) and that all four digits are pronounced individually.

一九七五年四月二十五 (号／日)	April 25th, 1975
二〇〇八年八月八 (号／日)	August 8th, 2008 (auspicious date for the start of the 2008 Beijing Olympics)

hao

number/day of month

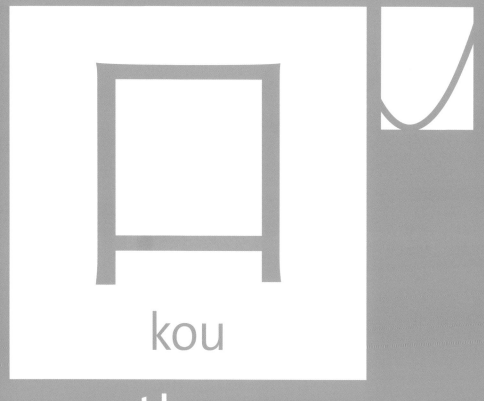

kou

mouth

shang

above/on

上 and its counterpart 下 *xia* (pg. 178) are two of the most commonly used characters.

上 means *above* or *up* when used with some locations, and *in* or *on* with others.

在天上   (up) in the sky
tian

wang上   on the Internet

As a verb 上 not only means *rise* or *climb* (as in 上shan, *to climb a mountain*), but also *go* when used with habitual actions.

上ban   to go to work
上学   to go to school

Finally, 上 means *last* when used with time expressions. It may be useful to think of time as being a river (with both *upstream* and *downstream*) to remember this interesting way of thinking about past and future events. The boat of life bobs downstream towards the future, leaving upstream events in the past.

上个星期   last week
下个星期   next week

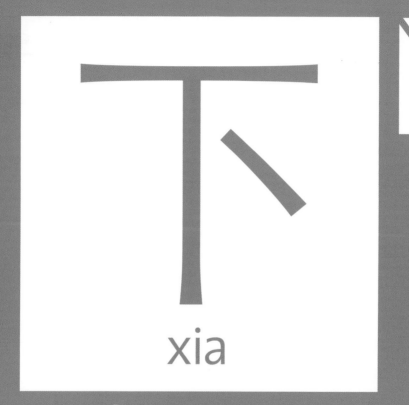

xia

under

下 also has many meanings. Notice that both 下 and 上 are ideographs (see pg. 17 中) pointing down and up respectively.

下 means *below* or *under* when used with locations.

在shafa下mian   under the sofa

As a verb, 下 means both *descend* and *alight* (from a vehicle), but also *fall*, as with precipitation.

下che   to get out of a vehicle

下yu   to rain

As an antonym of 上, 下 means *to get off*, or *to quit* a habitual action.

下ban   to get off work

一下 means *a little* or *briefly* when used with verbs.

请deng一下。   Please wait a little bit.

ri

sun/day

Translate the following into Chinese:

They can speak Chinese.

••

They speak Chinese very well.

••

How do you say (it) in English?

••

Can you make Chinese food?

••

How was the USA?

••

guo

to exceed

As a verb, 过 means *to go across* or *to pass*. It is often used with time expressions to mean *to spend*, or *to celebrate*.

过生日 <small>sheng</small>	to celebrate one's birthday
过年	to celebrate the New Year
过来	to come over

As an unstressed particle, 过 indicates or emphasizes past experience. Note that 没 (pg. 72), rather than 不, is used in negative sentences with this construction.

你去过日ben吗?	Have you been to Japan?
我没去过。	No, I haven't.

不过 is primarily used in two ways:

1. As a conjunction similar to *but*.

我想去, <small>xiang</small>	I want to go,
不过没有qian。	but I don't have money.

2. As an adverb similar to *merely* or *only*.

她不过是个学生。	She is only a student.

xiang

to think

想 is often used in front of a verb to express desire or intention.

我想去美国。	I want to go to the United States.
你想不想去?	Do you want to go?
你想喝什么?	What do you want to drink?

It is also used in compound verbs referring to thoughts and feelings.

我想不起来你的mingzi。	I can't remember your name.
我好想你!	I miss you!
hui想	to remember/to reflect on
想不dao	unexpected

This character is composed of an *eye* 目 examining a *tree* 木 to give the phonetic reading, and a *heart* 心 *xin* (pg. 154), the seat of emotion and thought, to give the meaning.

ming

bright/future

昨

zuo

yesterday

jin

present

In addition to *today* 今天 *jintian*, 今 can be combined with *year* to form a similar construction. 明 is also used this way. Note that *last year* is 去年 and not *昨年.

今天/明天	today/tomorrow
今年/明年	this year/next year
今后	from now on
今日	today (formal)
今wan	tonight
今zao	this morning

189

tian

day/heaven

While the character 天 means *sky* or *heaven*, its more common meanings of *day* and *season* are perhaps more useful for the beginning learner.

昨天/今天/明天	yesterday/today/tomorrow
星期天/星期日	Sunday
chun天	Spring
xia天	Summer
qiu天	Autumn
dong天	Winter
天qi	weather
bai天	daytime
liao天	to chat
天anmen	Tiananmen
天文	astrology

This character is a pictograph of the expanse of space above a person 大. 天 also means *talent* or *ability* (something granted by heaven) in certain compounds.

天cai	genius
天fen	talent, ability
天生 sheng	natural, innate

都

dou/du

all

都 is an adverb in Chinese that is used to mean *both* or *all*. It is used directly before the verb.

他们都学中文。	They all study Chinese.
大家都吃了吗?	Has everyone eaten?
你喜欢中国还是日ben? xi huan	Do you like China or Japan?
我都喜欢。	I like both.

No or *none* can be expressed with 都 and negation.

我们都没去过日ben。	None of us have been to Japan. (lit., *We all have not been to Japan.*)

都 is pronounced du when it means *city*.

shou都	capital
beijing是中国的shou都。	Beijing is the capital of China.
国ji都shi	an international city

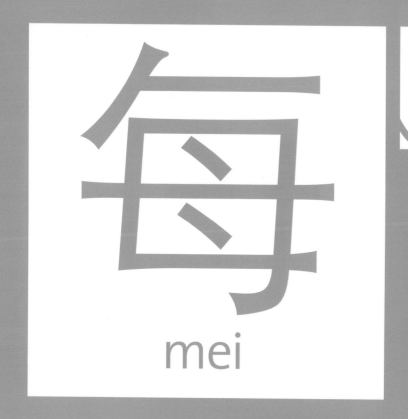

mei

every

每 is composed of the characters for *mother* 母 and *person* 人 to convey that *every* person has a mother. 每 is usually accompanied by 都, and is used in expressions that mean *each* or *every*. The beginning learner will probably be most familiar with 每天 *every day*. As with other time and frequency expressions, 每天 precedes the verb in Chinese:

他每天都学xi。	He studies every day. (lit., *He every day studies*.)
我每天都九点上ban。	I go to work every day at 9:00.
每年	every year
每ci	every time
每个人都喜欢他。 xi huan	Everyone likes him.
每个星期	every week
每个月	every month
每家饭dian	every restaurant

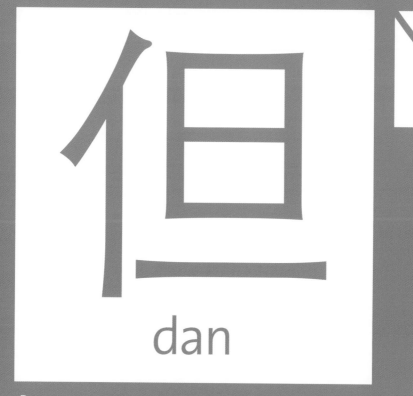

dan

but

Both 但是 and 可是 mean *but* or *however*. The former is a bit more emphatic than the latter.

他会说英语,	He can speak English,
但是他不会说法语。	but he can't speak French.
我想去中国,	I want to go to China,
但是我没有qian。	but I don't have any money.
你去过中国,	You've been to China,
但是没去过日ben, 对不对?	but not Japan, right?

哪

na/nei

which

哪 is the question word that corresponds to the demonstratives introduced on pg. 67. As *what* or *which*, it is used with a classifier in much the same way as 这 and 那.

你在哪儿?	Where are you?
你是哪国人?	Which country are you from?
你要哪ben书?	Which book do you need?
哪个人?	Which person?
哪个是你的?	Which one is yours?
那个是我的。	That one is mine.

Where, 哪里, is used as a modest response to a compliment (lit., *Where do you get such an idea?*).

你中文说得很好!	You speak Chinese very well!
哪里, 哪里。	Not at all.

As with all question words, the question particle 吗 cannot be used. 哪, like 那, is sometimes pronounced *nei* with no change in meaning.

yao

to want/to need

要 can be interpreted as *to want* or *to need* depending on context. It can be followed by a noun to express desire.

我要kafei, 不要cha。 I want coffee, not tea.

It can also combine with a verb to express intent for the future.

他要学中文。 He wants to study Chinese.

我要吃beijingkaoya。 I want to eat Peking duck.

When used with the second person pronoun 你, 要 takes on the tone of an imperative command.

你要小心! Be careful!

不要 is used for negative imperatives. As with English, the subject is often dropped.

不要吃! Don't eat it!

mai

to buy

yu

language

hua

speech/language

Both 语 and 话 are characters dealing with speech or language, as implied by the radical for speech 讠.

语 (*five* 五 *mouths* 口 talking) can be used in much the same way as 文. While 文 implies written language and 语 implies spoken language, they are often used interchangeably, as in 英文／英语 *English language*.

The Chinese language is called different things by people living in different places, and with a massive population that speaks dozens of languages and dialects, there is considerable debate regarding these terms. For the foreign language student, 中文 is the most general term for the *Chinese language*, and han语 is often used instead of 中文 to specify spoken *Mandarin Chinese*, as opposed to Cantonese or other dialects. 国语 is used in Taiwan and hua语 is used in Singapore to refer to this spoken language.

While 中国话 refers to spoken *Chinese language* in general, putong话 (lit., *common speech*) is the technical term for Standard Mandarin Chinese.

话 also appears in other compounds involving *speech* or *message*.

dian话   telephone
shen话   a myth
huang话   a lie

hai

still/also

Chinese only has one word for both *still* and *yet*. 还 always precedes the verb in this usage.

我们还在这儿。	We're still here.
你还学中文吗?	Are you still studying Chinese?

Still becomes *yet* when it precedes a negated verb.

你有没有女pengyou?	Do you have a girlfriend?
还没有。	Not yet.

还 is also used to introduce additional information about a subject similar to *also* in English.

他会说中文,	He can speak Chinese;
还会说fa语。	he also can speak French.

还是, *or*, is used to distinguish between two or more possibilities.

你去, 还是她去?	Are you going or is she?
你喝hongcha还是喝kafei?	Do you drink black tea, or do you drink coffee?

See page 115 for information about the idiomatic usage of 还可以.

shei/shui

who

Like 什么 and 哪里, 谁 is a question word that is inserted in the location of the answer it requests.

她是谁?	Who is she?
她是王太太。 wang	She's Mrs. Wang.

谁 can be placed at the beginning of a sentence (similar to English word order) to add emphasis.

谁是你的laoshi?	Who is your teacher?

Who becomes the possessive pronoun and adjective *whose* with the addition of the particle 的.

这是谁的?	Whose is this?
那是我的。	That's mine.

As with other content questions such as 什么, 谁 becomes *everyone* or *no one* when combined with 也 or 都.

谁都说英文很nan。	Everyone says English is hard.
谁也不会zuo这个gongzuo。	No one can do this job.

谁 can be pronounced either shei or shui with no change in meaning.

nin

you (formal)

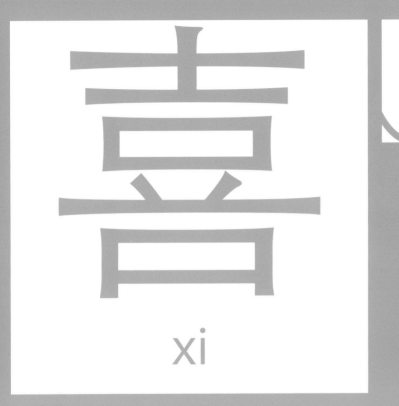

xi

happy

huan

to like

喜 and 欢 are used in a variety of expressions that convey joy and good will. gong喜 *congratulations* is used for accomplishments such as weddings and job promotions, and gong喜facai (lit., *congratulations and prosperous wishes*) is the traditional greeting at Chinese New Year. 欢ying (often repeated twice) is the expression used for welcoming someone to a home or business.

gong喜facai!	Happy Chinese New Year!
欢ying, 欢ying!	Welcome!

喜欢 is a useful two-character verb that means *to like* or *to be fond of*. 喜欢 can be combined with 什么 and a noun,

你喜欢什么yanse?	What color do you like?

or with a verb to inquire about tastes and hobbies:

你喜欢吃什么菜?	What kind of food do you like to eat?
她喜欢看什么书?	What kind of books does she like to read?

sheng

to be born

生 is derived from a pictograph of a growing plant. 生日 is a literal equivalent for *birthday*.

你的生日是几月几号?	When is your birthday?
我的生日是四月二十八号。	My birthday is April 28th.

生 is also used as a suffix for certain common nouns, such as yi生 *doctor*, 学生 *student*, and xian生 *sir/Mr.*

他是yi生。	He is a doctor.
我们不是学生。	We are not students.

生 is also used idiomatically with certain things that grow or are produced, and is an adjective that means *raw* or *uncooked*. *Draft beer* is 生pijiu in Chinese since it is often unpasteurized.

生yi	business
生chan	to produce/to manufacture
我喜欢生pijiu。	I like draft beer.

zuo

to do/to make

216

做 is a widely used verb. When used for *to do* it can be used interchangeably with the slightly more informal gan.

你在做什么?	What are you doing?
你在gan什么?	What are you doing?

When asking about someone's occupation, *to do* is used as it is in English.

你做什么gongzuo?	What do you do? (What is your job?)

做 also means *to make*. Chinese meals typically consist of a staple food 饭 such as rice or noodles, along with several side dishes 菜. While 做饭 is *to cook rice* or *cooking* in a very general sense, 做菜 implies a more refined type of meal preparation. When complimenting or referring to someone's cooking, you should always use 做菜 rather than 做饭.

我喜欢做菜,	I like to cook,
但是做得不好。	but I don't cook well.
你会做中国菜吗?	Can you make Chinese food?

sui

human age

Congratulations! You have learned over 100 Chinese characters! Since over 90 percent of the language is composed of some 1000 characters, you are well on your way! Use colored pencils or markers to increase the mnemonic effectiveness of these final review exercises.

Match the following characters into pairs according to common tones. (There is more than one correct answer).

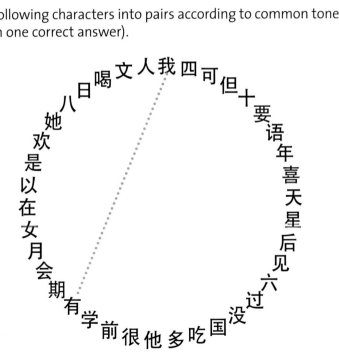

Color the following grid with the correct tone color for each character.
A number will appear when you are finished.

里	个	每	过	很	这	是	有
菜	月	期	八	七	星	九	看
我	年	多	国	文	那	以	美
饭	日	都	今	听	说	人	哪
怎	样	四	五	可	天	什	十
明	得	她	中	他	家	为	小
会	点	在	上	少	下	时	大

TONAL COUSINS

With only 460 possible syllable sounds and five to six thousand characters, modern Chinese has a great number of homophones. It also has many occurrences of what I call "tonal cousins." A set of tonal cousins is a group of two or more characters that share the exact same syllable pronounced in different tones. For example, 是 *to be* and 十 *ten* are tonal cousins in that they are pronounced exactly the same way but in different tones. The beginning learner may find it useful to learn these cousins in groups. Write (preferably in color) at least two tonal cousins discussed in this book for each of the syllables below:

shi ....   mei ....

jian ....   wen ....

yi ....   zuo ....

er ....   hao ....

xie ....   na ....

qi ....

FIRST TONE/RED

今	jin	present	188–189
七	qi	seven	139
她	ta	she	28–29
说	shuo	to speak	92–93
星	xing	star	146–147, 149
高	gao	tall	81
三	san	three	135

SECOND TONE/ORANGE

前	qian	before/front	105, 106
明	ming	bright/future	91, 186, 189
来	lai	to come	40–41, 43
国	guo	country	18–19
为	wei	for	79
男	nan	man	127, 129
不	bu	not	183, 169, 201
一	yi	one	132, 133
人	ren	person	22–23, 59, 65, 71
儿	er	son/child	69, 130–131
还	hai	still/also	206–207
学	xue	to study	59, 61, 91, 94
十	shi	ten	142–143

时	shi	time	61, 71, 111, 116–117, 119
什	shen	what	74–75, 77, 79, 117
谁	shei/shui	who	208–209
没	mei	without	33, 72–73, 183
文	wen	writing/culture/language	19, 90–91, 205
年	nian	year	160, 189
昨	zuo	yesterday	187
您	nin	you	210
零	ling	zero	143

THIRD TONE/GREEN

也	ye	also	77, 120–121, 209
美	mei	beauty	20–21
买	mai	to buy	202
每	mei	every	194–195
少	shao	few	56–57
五	wu	five	137
好	hao	good	15, 52–53
喜	xi	happy	211, 213
有	you	to have	33, 70–71, 73, 123
怎	zen	how	165, 166–167

上	shang	above/on	105, 176–177, 179
后	hou	after/back	105, 107
再	zai	again	86–87
现	xian	appear	108–109
问	wen	to ask	80, 83
是	shi	to be	12–13, 27, 49, 55, 111, 197, 207
会	hui	to be able	158–159
大	da	big	15, 55, 58–59, 61, 103
但	dan	but	196–197
候	hou	climate/time	118–119
对	dui	correct	162–163
日	ri	day/sun	173, 180, 215
菜	cai	dish/vegetable	45, 126
做	zuo	to do/to make	216–217
过	guo	to exceed	182–183
在	zai	to exist	17, 32–33, 109, 125
为	wei	for	78–79
四	si	four	136
去	qu	to go	42–43
半	ban	half	112–113

上	shang	above/on	*see* 上
生	sheng	to be born	*see* 生
日	ri	day	*see* 日
不	bu	not	27, 50, 89, 133
的	de	*particle*	15, 38–39, 51, 157, 169, 209
吗	ma	*particle*	24–25, 50, 73, 199
呢	ne	*particle*	25, 33, 34–35
了	le	*particle*	100, 103
得	de	*particle*	168–169
过	guo	to pass	79, 183
们	men	*plural suffix*	15, 30–31
儿	er	son/child	69, 111, 131
候	hou	time	117, 118, 119
个	ge	unit	65, 89, 113
么	me	what	67, 69, 75, 77, 79, 117, 167

GRAMMAR INDEX

AUDIO TRACK LISTING

DISC 1

DISC 2

243

ABOUT THE AUTHOR

Nathan Dummitt received his BA from the University of Illinois at Champaign. He lived and worked in Kumamoto, Japan, for three years and became interested in the etymology and development of the Chinese and Japanese languages. He currently teaches Chinese and Mathematics at Columbia Preparatory School in New York City.